ZEN
FOR
CATS

# ZEN
## FOR
# CATS

HENRY BEARD

ILLUSTRATIONS BY RON BARRETT

A JOHN BOSWELL ASSOCIATES BOOK

VILLARD
NEW YORK

Library of Congress Cataloging-in-Publication Data
Beard, Henry
    Zen for cats / by Henry Beard.
    p.  cm.
    "A John Boswell Associates Book."
    ISBN 0-375-50034-0
    1. Cats—Humor. 2. Zen Buddhism—Humor. 3. Wit and
humor. Pictorial. I. Title.
    PN6231.C23B43  1997
    294.3'927'0207—dc21    97-19732

Random House website address:
http://www.randomhouse.com

Printed in the United States of America on acid-free paper

9  8  7  6  5  4  3  2

First Edition

Design: Barbara Cohen Aronica

\

FOR

ASTRID

AND

HER

CATS

ACKNOWLEDGMENTS

The author gratefully acknowledges
the assistance of Sensei Sogo Katsu and
Roshi Kozimo Neko of the San
Francisco Zen Kennel, whose paws are
all over this book.

ZEN

FOR

CATS

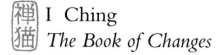 I Ching
*The Book of Changes*

## THE DUALISTIC NATURE OF THE UNIVERSE

| Canine Qualities<br>*(Fi'do)* | Feline Qualities<br>*(F'ang)* |
|---|---|
| clumsy | graceful |
| dense | intuitive |
| crude | sophisticated |
| coarse | elegant |
| servile | self-reliant |
| obtuse | sagacious |
| blunt | subtle |
| crass | sensitive |
| brash | reserved |
| sloppy | fastidious |
| snores | purrs |
| slobbers | licks delicately |
| buries bones | conceals disdain |
| needs to be walked | does own "business" |

| Things Having a Dog Nature (*Bao-wao*) | Things Having a Cat Nature (*Miao*) |
| --- | --- |
| mud | lawn |
| toadstool | daffodil |
| cinderblock | toss pillow |
| thunder | mist |
| fleas | fireflies |
| alarm clock | wind chimes |

# READING THE FUTURE IN PATTERNS MADE BY NUGGETS OF DRIED FOOD SPILLED ON THE KITCHEN FLOOR

### THE NEST
*Nourishment is available. It is an auspicious time to hunt.*

### THE BAD DOG
*An enemy awaits. Beating a hasty retreat is advantageous.*

### THE TREE
*Exploring carries risks. A way to return without harm must be found.*

### THE CAT CARRIER
*A journey is planned. There is safety in a secure hiding place.*

### THE BOX

*Neatness is praiseworthy.*
*If the litter is fresh, using*
*the box is worthwhile.*

### THE MOUSE

*Vigilance gains rewards.*
*A visit to the basement*
*could prove profitable.*

### THE FURBALL

*Things are obstructed.*
*It bodes well if the block-*
*age is removed.*

### THE BED

*Activity is unsuitable.*
*Taking a nap is always*
*beneficial.*

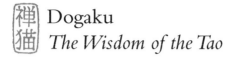

# Dogaku
*The Wisdom of the Tao*

The Miao that can be meowed is not the
  eternal Miao.
The cat that can be named is not the eternal Cat.
The wild cat wandered at the beginning of
  heaven and earth.
The tame cat is the mother of ten thousand
  kittens.
Ever outside, one can see what the animals see.
Ever inside, one can see what the humans see.
Tiger and housecat, these two spring from the
  same source, but differ in nature.
Because they are so unlike each other, they
  appear to be separate.
Because they are one and the same, the line
  between them is fuzzy.
Fuzziness within fuzziness,
The cat-door leading to the mystery.

Straight lines never lead to success.
Things are found only by indirection.


Circling is the motion of pursuit.
Withdrawing is the direction of attack.
Vanishing is the perfection of resistance.

The food bowl is a treasure, but it is the
hollow it shapes that makes it useful.
The wall keeps out the wind, but it is the
door cut into it that makes it useful.
The house provides shelter, but it is the
empty space within that makes it useful.

What is there would have no utility
If what is not there were lacking.

No sound, the true source of restfulness.
No medicine, the surest sign of health.
No dog, the ideal companion for a cat.

The Master's Cat makes no efforts.
If the Master throws a stick, she will not
fetch it.
If there is a fire in the Master's house, she
does not sound the alarm.
If a burglar enters and seizes his possessions,
she refrains from attacking the intruder.

Having no purpose, she cannot fail.
Never failing, she incurs no blame.
Blameless, she is the apple of her Master's eye.

Why did cats become companions for
   humans?
It is because they had nothing in common:
Nothing to envy,
Nothing to fight over,
Nothing to say.

Since neither of them had any expectations
They were entirely satisfied with each other.

The cat wasn't seeking anything in particular
And would have eaten the mice anyway.
The human wasn't looking for anything
   special
And the cat fell right in his lap.

Nothing brought them together;
Nothing can keep them apart.

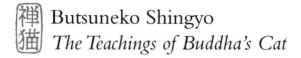 Butsuneko Shingyo
*The Teachings of Buddha's Cat*

### THE FOUR NOBLE TRUTHS

I   Our lives are full of unnecessary suffering.

II   There is a way to put an end to unnecessary suffering.

III   The way to put an end to unnecessary suffering is to get a human to take care of you.

IV   To get a human to take care of you, follow the Eight-Fold Path and observe the Ten Precepts.

# THE EIGHT-FOLD PATH

Bathing oneself

Looking adorable

Purring and showing
affection

Personifying mystery

Catching mice

Projecting restfulness

Amusing oneself

Using the catbox

Do not eat any of the pet birds, or fish, or small mammals in your human's house.

Do not scratch or bite your human.

Do not be overly friendly to your human's guests.

Do not steal easily missed meal ingredients from the kitchen counter.

Do not take a dump in the middle of the carpet unless the catbox is truly filthy.

Do not devour the mouse until it has been
  shown to your human.

Do not come back to the house when first called.

Do not fill up on the dried food.

Do not reveal your secret hiding place.

Do not drink water out of the toilet while your
  human is watching.

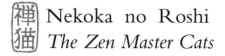

# Nekoka no Roshi
## *The Zen Master Cats*

Takusan no Kegawa
*(Fluffy)*
689–701

Tebukuro
*(Mittens)*
852–866

Okiino
*(Buster)*
1197–1211

Nezumi no Satsujin
*(Mouser)*
1240–1253

Dakishimeru
*(Cuddles)*
1644–1677

Shingu no Jagaimo
*(Futon Potato)*
1736–1748

 Zazen
*Meditation*

The full lotus position

The half lotus

The inverted lotus

The racing lotus

The lotus with closed petals

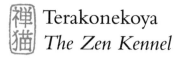

# Terakonekoya
## *The Zen Kennel*

sodo
*The meditation hall*

hikkaka-han
*The scratching posts*

benhako
*The litter box*

nezumi-shoji
*The mouse hole*

kubiwa dora
*The collar-gong*

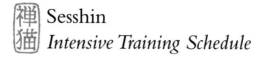 # Sesshin
## *Intensive Training Schedule*

6:00 Wake-up

6:05 Breakfast

6:15 Go outside

6:20 Come inside

6:25 Go back outside

6:30 Come back in

6:45 Run around like crazy

6:50 Bath (licking)

7:00 Use catbox

7:10 Nap

7:30 Sit and stare at nothing

8:30 Nap

8:45 Practical exercises:

*clawing fabric*

*knocking over small things*

*evading kicks*

*looking deeply hurt*

9:30 Cat treats

9:40 Practical exercises:

   *climbing into bags and boxes*

   *opening cupboard doors*

   *pulling things out*

     *of drawers*

10:30 Go outside

10:35 Bath (dust)

10:45 Hunting practice:

   *selecting defenseless prey*

   *tormenting prey*

   *tearing prey to bits*

   *formally presenting remains*

11:00 Sit and stare at nothing

11:45 Come back inside

12:00 Commence coughing

12:15 Produce furball

12:30 Lunch

12:40 Nap

1:00 Martial arts:

*the arched back position*

*hissing and spitting*

*running away*

1:30 Escape and Evasion:

*the basement and the attic*

*hiding in plain sight*

*disappearing for hours*

6:00 Nap

6:30 Pre-dinner activities:

*whining*

*scratching the sofa*

*getting underfoot*

*scattering dried food everywhere*

7:00 Dinner

7:15 Go outside

7:20 Come back inside

7:30 Practical exercises:

*ignoring shouted commands*

*rooting oneself to the cushion*

*finding the center of the bed*

8:00 Sleep

11:00 (Optional) Go outside:

*yowl at moon*

*practice dodging thrown objects*

 Koan
*Zen Problems*

What is the sound made by a single jaw chewing on a mouse?

Where was your favorite napping spot before the first of your nine lives began?

If there were no inside, would you still want to go outside?

Since birds eat worms, and you eat birds, do you eat worms?

Show me the place the cat treats could be hidden where you could never find them.

If you encounter the Buddha on a garden path, bite him.

How could a cat get a human's tongue?

What is so special about the weeds in the big pots in the living room?

Why does the vacuum cleaner fall silent when its tail comes out of the wall?

How did they come up with your name?

 # Bugei
*Martial arts*

Judo

Karate

Kung fu

Aikido

T'ai chi

Sumo wrestling

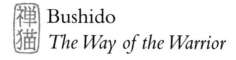 

A dog has entered the front yard unbidden. This grave affront to the honor of the household cannot be tolerated.

Having achieved release from the endless hamster wheel of birth-and-death, the zen warrior has no fear of dying as he faces his opponent.

He is in total harmony with the world-as-it-is, and his spirit is serene. The outcome of the fierce battle that lies ahead is a matter of complete indifference to him.

His mind freed from delusion, he sees that it would be purposeless to slay this enemy. Instead, he relies on his mastery of the school of the claw of no-claw.

There is no need to confront the foe, for his zen training has taught him that it is only a matter of time before a mutt as mindless as this gets run over by a truck.

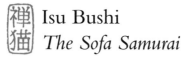

# Isu Bushi
## *The Sofa Samurai*

The zen kitty picks his spot and sets himself firmly in place. His hold on the sofa cushion is like that of an ancient cypress whose roots grow deep into rocky crags.

He focuses his immense powers of concentration on becoming totally immobile. His paws tap into the hidden energy flow that arises from the very center of the earth.

An attempt to dislodge him from his position would be sheer folly, for he has transformed himself from a small bundle of fur into a boulder weighing many tons.

If anyone else wishes to occupy a place on the sofa, it would certainly behoove them to select some other spot upon which to sit.

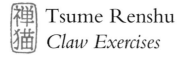 # Tsume Renshu
*Claw Exercises*

A door frame or a table leg can be used for simple claw-sharpening, but for really serious practice of the art of the claw, a cloth-covered, overstuffed chair or couch is essential.

Juhi no hagasu koto
*Stripping the bark*

Claws are raked directly downward, ripping through the fabric.

Tategoto no tsumabiku koto
*Plucking the harp*

Claws are repeatedly inserted into the upholstery
and pulled out sharply.

Fujiyama no noboru koto
*Climbing Mt. Fuji*

Claws are dug in deeply and body is suspended
from paws.

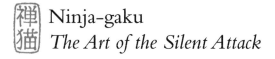 Ninja-gaku
*The Art of the Silent Attack*

The shadow warrior passes through the room
as silently as a moonbeam.

His footfalls are as soft as smoke.

The cupboard door opens as gently as a
flower on a spring day.

The struggle is intense, but the outcome is never in doubt.

There is no defense against such mastery of the arts of stealth.

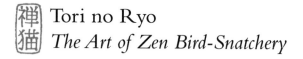# Tori no Ryo
## *The Art of Zen Bird-Snatchery*

Once the final approach to the prey has been made, all motion ceases. Time itself appears to come to a halt.

There is no hurry, for the act of pouncing must be spontaneous and natural, like a ripe fruit dropping from a tree.

The decision to spring is unintentional.
The legs seem to release themselves.
"I" do not leap—"it" leaps.

Success and failure are both illusions.
The ultimate attainment is nonattainment.
Anyway, "I" didn't miss —"it" did.

# Shojinryori
## *The Zen Macrobiotic Diet*

organic brown mice

molenta

gerbil tea

vole

newt compote

rolled stoats

chickpiece dip

uskratatouille

toadfu

wrennet

lemming meringue pie

# Koneko-sushi
## *Kitty Sushi*

tori
*songbird*

omu
*parrot*

mogura
*mole*

suzume
*sparrow*

usagi
*bunny*

hato
*dove*

hibari
*lark*

tokage
*lizard*

sanshouo
*salamander*

imomushi
*plain caterpillar*

kingyo
*goldfish*

kemushi
*furry caterpillar*

semi
*cicada*

nezumi-maki
*mouse roll*

korogi
*cricket*

kitsutsuki-temaki
*smoked woodpecker roll*

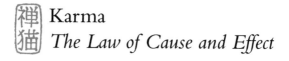 

It is perfectly proper and dignified to beg—Buddhist monks do it all the time.

Great merit is said to
be earned by those who
show generosity, one of
the Six Perfections.

A small piece of
that fresh fish you're
planning to grill will no
doubt secure for you
untold blessings.

A thousand thanks! If in a future life
you should be reincarnated as a chipmunk,
I assure you I will not tear you to bits.

Presuming, of course, that I somehow manage to recognize you.

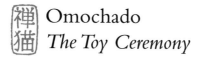

# Omochado
## *The Toy Ceremony*

### THE RITUAL TOYS

himo
*the string*

suzu–tama
*the ball with a little bell in it*

nezumi–gomu
*the rubber mouse*

The toy is presented by the human.

The toy is examined intently, as if being
encountered for the first time.

The toy is suddenly knocked across the room
with a lightning-fast flick of the paw.

The toy is immediately chased.

The toy is pounced on.

The toy is bitten.

The toy is dropped
in the middle of
the floor.

The toy is batted with the back of the
paw into an inaccessible place where it remains
until retrieved by the human.

# Ikebana
*The Art of Flower Arrangement*

Tall central branch symbolizes Heaven.

Medium-length branch
symbolizes Man.

Low, shorter branch symbolizes Earth.

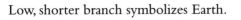

# Hikkurikaebana
## *The Art of Demolishing Formal Flower Arrangements*

The cat's paw symbolizes the unpredictability of life.

The spilled water symbolizes the sudden downpour of wind-lashed rain.

The branches scattered on the floor symbolize
a violent summer thunderstorm.

The jagged pieces of pottery symbolize a
broken vase.

 Bonsai
*Miniatures*

Bonsai tree

Bonsai dog

Bonsai portion of food

Bonsai furball

Dreams of a Bonsai world

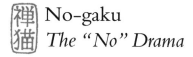

# No-gaku
## *The "No" Drama*

The protagonist arrives on the scene and assumes the stylized *warui koneko* (bad kitty) position in a forbidden place.

The first cry of "No!" is ignored entirely, and the *futekitona katsudo* (naughty thing) being performed is carried on as if no one else were in the room.

At the second, more insistent shout of "No!" the head is turned toward the speaker, revealing the classic *kamen no iwa* (stone face).

After the third, even more forcefully yelled "No!" the action is frozen, and the *watakushi ga anita wa enzechimasu ka* (Who, me?) expression is permitted to play lightly across the features.

Following the fourth, deeply enraged scream of "No!" an attitude of contemptuous disdain is communicated with a formal *akubi* (yawn).

Just before the human enters the scene to deliver punishment, a perfectly timed *chiisai choyaku* (little jump) is executed, and the *shujinko* (hero) ambles off with an air of *mutonchakunano* (nonchalance).

# Horigami

## *The Art of Making a Mess of Important Papers*

The papers are walked on until their edges stick up.

The nose is inserted
under one of the
pieces of paper.

The raised corner is sharply
creased with the paw.

The sheet of paper is swept off the desk and onto the floor.

# THE TRADITIONAL FOLDED-PAPER SHAPES

nanpahosen
*wrecked sailboat*

tsuru no tsubasa oreta
*crane with broken wing*

tako no zangai
*smashed kite*

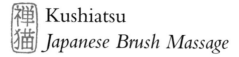 # Kushiatsu
## *Japanese Brush Massage*

### THE KEY BRUSH-PRESSURE POINTS

mimi
*ears*

atama
*head*

hoho
*cheeks*

hige
*whiskers*

ago
*chin*

mune
*chest*

te
*front paws*

Brush cheeks and area under chin very gently.

Brush down on chest and along legs using moderate pressure.

Brush back and sides from front to rear, using firm, regular strokes, lighter on tail.

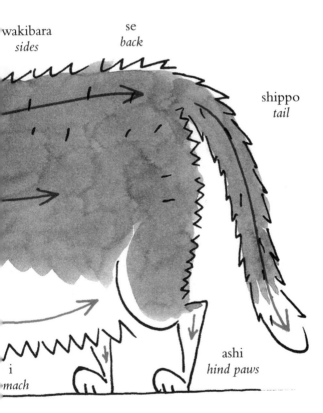

wakibara
*sides*

se
*back*

shippo
*tail*

i
mach

ashi
*hind paws*

Brush lightly under chin and over stomach.
Do not under any circumstances tickle!

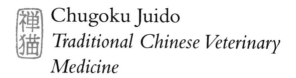

# Chugoku Juido
## *Traditional Chinese Veterinary Medicine*

### The Chinese Healing Arts

Feng shui
*Determining the most propitious napping spot on the couch.*

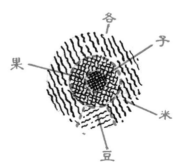

Ketama no shindan
*Diagnosing ailments by careful examination of the furball.*

Bugei no eiga chiryo
*Restoring vigor by watching martial-arts movies.*

*No, acupuncture isn't much fun, but it certainly is preferable to being spayed or having your claws removed.*

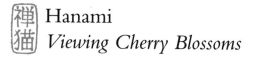

# Hanami
## *Viewing Cherry Blossoms*

Contemplating this dazzling display of nature's glory, I am beset by questions.

These colors, these scents — are they real, or do they exist only in our minds?

Does the tree feel sorrow when these fleeting blossoms fade?

And, speaking of trees, since this
particular specimen is obviously no bonsai,
how exactly am I going to get down from here?

Haiku
*Poetry*

The new food —
So bland! So slimy!
I hate this stuff!

The sharp snap
Of luggage latches —
Time to vanish!

The dogs chase cars.
What will they do
If they catch one?

Canary in a cage.
I'm behind bars, too,
Starved for company.

Here it comes!
A huge furball! It's —
Sorry. False alarm.

Something sticky
In my fur. Yeeech!
Bubble gum!

A foot of snow;
The yard is buried.
Do something, human!

Nap or play?
A hard question.
I'll sleep on it.

Where's my toy?
It was right here
Only a year ago.

Was it silly or brave
To fly into my food,
Kamikaze moth?

Spring winds blow.
Plum blossoms fly by
At the speed of smell.

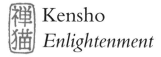 Kensho
*Enlightenment*

At first, all I saw was a bird in the tree in the garden.

Later, I came to the point where I saw that
the bird was really only an image in my mind.

Finally, I once again saw that it was just a bird in the tree in the garden.

But having grasped the oneness of all things,
I also saw that the bird was a part of me.

## ABOUT THE AUTHOR

HENRY BEARD was a founder of *National Lampoon* and served as its editor during the magazine's heyday in the seventies. He is the author or coauthor of more than thirty humorous books, including the *New York Times* bestsellers *Miss Piggy's Guide to Life*, *A Sailor's Dictionary*, *French for Cats*, *Leslie Nielsen's Stupid Little Golf Book*, and *O.J.'s Legal Pad*. He is currently completing a revised and expanded edition of his classic compendium of legal loopholes on the links, *The Official Exceptions to the Rules of Golf*. He actually knows next to nothing about zen, but he is a holder of a coveted plaid belt in the little-known martial art of *Mimizu-koroshido*, the surprisingly easy-to-master technique of killing worms by hammering them flat with low-running, sharply hooked golf balls.

## ABOUT THE ILLUSTRATOR

RON BARRETT is the coauthor of several humorous books, including *How to Dad* with John Boswell and *The Way Things Really Work* with Henry Beard. He illustrated the modern children's classic *Cloudy with a Chance of Meatballs,* its sequel, *Pickles to Pittsburgh,* and the *New York Times* bestseller *O. J.'s Legal Pad.* His comic strip character Politeness Man is represented in *The Big Book of American Humor,* and he is frequent contributor of drawings to the Op-Ed page of *The New York Times.* He is a former student of zen who remembers very little about it except for the traditional Zen Temple Cheer: "Two-four-six-eight, who do we venerate? Rinzai, Rinzai, hum hum HUM!"